HANS DEN HARTOG JAGER

THE ESSENTIAL VAN GOGH

KRÖLLER-MÜLLER
MUSEUM

Content

Introduction

Great artists, truly great artists, live for hundreds of years. Sometimes through their work, sometimes through their reputation, usually through a mixture of the two. Say »Picasso« and everyone thinks of pictures of a woman with an impossible nose and triangular chin – but they also see the virile artist with his piercing eyes and Julius Caesar hair style. And who doesn't know the Mona Lisa's smile, painted by Leonardo da Vinci. He is the prototype man of genius, both many-sided and playful, designing an aeroplane with his left hand while with the other he paints a Madonna.

Then there is Vincent Willem van Gogh (1853–1890). His reputation is less enviable. For almost a hundred years artists, museum folk and gallery owners have spoken of the so-called »Van Gogh syndrome«. They're all afraid of it. The Van Gogh syndrome represents the angst that in our own lifetime, possibly right here in our midst, there is a major, visionary artist at work, whom we totally fail to recognize. Look at Van Gogh's story. He agonized with reality, wrestled with the world, painted in solitude. Hardly any of his work was exhibited during his lifetime. Many an artist would hang up his brush upon the proverbial willow tree for less.

And yet, it is hard to blame his contemporaries for this under-evaluation. True, Van Gogh was notoriously misunderstood; indeed, his story is unique in the history of art. Seldom has an artist developed his talents and attained such heights in so brief a span of time. Not until he was 27 years old did Van Gogh seriously begin to draw. Then followed a five-year warming–up period; he practised, he mastered techniques.

In 1885 he was ready to begin on a series of paintings which raised him in one breath to a place among the great artists of all time. To say these works are brilliant, astounding, is an understatement. Not surprisingly, Van Gogh is often compared with a comet: for five brief years from 1885 to 1890, he lit up the sky above the world of art. If you weren't paying attention right then, you'd have missed him.

This makes the achievement of Mrs Helene Kröller-Müller, founder and namesake of the Kröller-Müller Museum, all the more remarkable. When she was taking a course in art history under the Dutch art historian H.P. Bremmer in 1907 she encountered the work of Van Gogh. Captivated by Art, she decided to use her sizeable capital to purchase paintings. She bought Corots and Millets, Picassos and Seurats, but above all work by Vincent van Gogh. The first Van Gogh she owned was Edge of a Wood from 1883; many were to follow. In total, in the space of about forty years, Mrs Kröller-Müller acquired around 165 drawings and 90 paintings by »Vincent«. This collection is the second largest and finest in the world, after that of the Van Gogh Museum in Amsterdam.

This book presents an extensive selection from the Kröller-Müller collection. All the biggies are here: The Potato Eaters, Terrace of a Café at Night (Place du Forum), Pink Peach Trees (Souvenir de Mauve), the Bridge at Arles (Pont de Langlois) and La Berceuse (Portrait of Mme Roulin). Thus the book honours Vincent van Gogh, but at the same time is a huge encouragement for every artist who today is working in solitude, polishing up a masterpiece. Just as Leonardo da Vinci and Picasso are the patron saints of anyone who is a genius, so is Vincent van Gogh the consoler of the unrecognized and misunderstood, the most human among the great artists. Undoubtedly, this explains some of his popularity although at the same time people recognize that such an extreme example of under-rating will probably never happen again. After all, those interested in art have taken heed of the »Van Gogh syndrome«. Van Gogh's work, all those sublime landscapes, still lifes, flowers and self-portraits are blazoned against the sky like an unending and overwhelming firework display.

The first Van Gogh that Mrs Kröller-Müller purchased was 'Edge of a Wood', from 1883

Edge of a Wood AUGUST–SEPTEMBER 1883

preliminary stages

One bright autumn morning in 1876 the congregation of the Methodist church in Richmond, Surrey, in the south of England, beheld an unknown figure mount the pulpit. Their »customary minister«, Mr T. Slade Jones, was ill that day and his place was taken by a 23-year-old Dutchman with red hair and a riveting gaze. Vincent van Gogh, for he was the young man, was nervous. It was his first sermon. Standing in the pulpit of the small wooden church he regaled his fellow-believers with a passionate narration, taking as text that mankind is a stranger upon the earth. Everyone's life, he tells them, is a pilgrimage through which they may be guided and supported by Jesus Christ. Then, towards the close of his sermon, Van Gogh produces a striking example. He describes in impassioned language, a »beautiful painting«. It is a landscape in the evening light with the sun sinking below the distant mountains. On the left a city can be seen; through the landscape a pilgrim trudges on his way. He has been travelling a long time and is weary. Then he meets a woman; she is dressed in black and to the pilgrim she seems like an angel. She tells him that his journey to reach the city will take »from sunrise to sundown«. And so, concluded the young preacher, is our life. We all have to travel along the path towards the horizon; let us pray that God will go with us in the shape of an angel.

As if Van Gogh knew what lay before him.

Much has been written about Vincent Willem van Gogh (1853-1890), art dealer, for a brief while lay preacher, and artist. In the twentieth century the story of his life assumed mammoth proportions – it became the sometimes melodramatic and moving tale of the misunder-

'We must all follow the road that leads to the horizon'

Lane of Poplars at Sunset   1884

'And I repeat: Millet is
father Millet, that is, the guide and mentor
in all things for young painters'

L'Angélus du Soir (after Millet)   1880

stood artist. But the emotions are stirred for yet another reason. Van Gogh had a remarkable faith in his own work and after his death it proved justified. This is a hugely appealing story: as if all Van Gogh's suffering was in due time redeemed. Or, to make it even more intriguing – did Van Gogh believe in himself so steadfastly because he knew that one day he would gain his just reward?

Wait a moment – how could he have known that?

Well of course he couldn't have. But reading Van Gogh's letters, following his career, and studying his paintings, one is inclined to believe he did know. Because for almost all his adult life Vincent van Gogh seems to have felt he was working on something supremely important.

We shall never know where that belief, that immense, excessive, fantastic self-confidence came from. Undoubtedly it had something to do with his religious faith, for Van Gogh believed firmly in God. But other things turned Van Gogh into someone who was endlessly seeking. He felt he didn't fit into his time and place, he had bitter conflicts with his parents, his love life proved deeply disappointing. So he was on a lifelong quest, a pilgrim towards the city on the horizon that he sketched for his congregation in the first sermon he gave. Initially, he believed the city to be the City of God and that he was called to preach to the poor and assist them in this way. Later it became a city of Art, an Olympus on earth. He was to write, »Try to grasp the essence of what the great artists, the serious masters say in their masterworks, you will find God there.« The quest for that God, whatever form he might take, is perhaps the quintessence of Van Gogh's work. And looking at his life as a whole, we are tempted to conclude: he had the perfect qualities.

Vincent Willem van Gogh was born on 30 March 1853 in Zundert, a little village in the southern Netherlands province of Brabant. His mother, Anna Cornelia Carbentus, was a housewife and an amateur artist and his father, Theodorus van Gogh was, like his father before him, a minister in the Dutch Reformed Church. Traditionally, however, the Van Gogh family had tended to be either Protestant ministers or art dealers. Theodorus, for instance, came from a family of eleven, and three of his siblings were art dealers. So no one was in the least surprised when Vincent quitted his secondary school in Tilburg before completing his education and joined the Hague branch of the art dealers Goupil & Co, where his uncle Vincent worked. This uncle 'Cent' was the most successful of the Van Gogh brothers who went in for art dealing. From small beginnings in a little shop, he prospered so well that his business was taken over by the French chain of art galleries and publishers Goupil & Cie. Goupil specialized in paintings as well as the production and sale of reproductions. Uncle Vincent became a partner in this prestigious company.

Initially, things looked rosy at Goupil's for young Vincent. Starting off as the youngest shop assistant he was transferred after four years, in June 1873 to London and about a year later, in October 1874, was sent to the head branch in Paris. But somewhere, on the way between The Hague, London and Paris, something went wrong. In December 1874 Vincent was sent back to London, only to return to Paris in May 1875. Then on 1 April 1876 he resigned from the firm.

There has been much speculation about Vincent van Gogh's remarkable *Werdegang*, or development, in his career as art dealer. His brother Theo's widow, Jo Bonger, made the suggestion in the introduction to the first edition of Vincent's *Collected Letters*, that when he was in London her brother-in-law had fallen in love with his landlady's daughter Eugenie Loyer, with an unhappy outcome. Yet his letters make no mention of this even though he left behind him a good nine hundred epistles. There is something else worth considering: from 1874 onwards Vincent was increasingly absorbed by that other calling of the Van Gogh family: religion. Thus we find him writing to his brother Theo in September 1875: »As for our portion in life, let us pray to become as the poor in the kingdom of God, the servants of God. We have not yet attained that however, for there are often planks before our eyes that we do not ourselves recognize. Let us pray that our eyes may see things simply, for then we shall become entirely pure and simple.«

In the years that were to follow he would often make utterances of this kind. Indeed, it looks as if his work as an art dealer increasingly presented problems for his faith and his yearning after simplicity. One of the many rumours that circulated about what Van Gogh was like as a young man is the one relating how he would even persuade customers not to   buy a particular work if the piece in question didn't meet his artistic standards.

But what should he do with his life?

It soon became clear that Vincent was utterly sincere in his quest for God – the minister's family recognized the symptoms. Scarcely had Vincent given in his notice before he returned to England. First he worked as a teaching assistant at a private school in Ramsgate, a resort on the south coast. Then he held a similar post in Isleworth, a working-class district on the outskirts of London. It looked as if Van Gogh had found his life's mission, in preaching and teaching. In his letters the tone became calmer and he recorded enthusiastically walks he had been on in the countryside. Nevertheless, the neurotic ground bass was never long absent. »But woe to me if I fail to preach the Gospel. If I did not set my sights on that, if I did not fix my hope and trust in Christ , I should be plunged into utter woe; but now I have gained courage.«

The reports from London seemed heartening, so his parents were shocked by how he looked when he came home for Christmas 1876. Vincent was in such a bad state both mentally and physically that they persuaded him not to return to London. They arranged a job for him in a bookstore in Dordrecht, a historic town near Rotterdam. But he was tormented by his calling to the ministry. He went to church every day, he worked on a translation of the Bible. And he drew.

Shortly after this Van Gogh's parents let him go to Amsterdam to study for the National Examinations – if he passed these he would be qualified to study Theology. But again he failed, only to set off for Brussels where he planned to follow a course as a lay preacher. He failed again.

So he must have been near despair when in November 1878 he decided to set off for the Borinage district in Belgium. He had failed as an art dealer, been called to be a minister of the Word but not succeeded on this path either. In a letter to Theo he reflects that he resembles the Apostle Paul, who before he began his missionary work spent three years »in Arabia«. Vincent wanted similarly to spend three years among the miners, in order to be able to return »with something worth listening to.«

The wildest stories are told about the one-and-a-half years that Vincent passed in the Borinage. Indeed, they become ever more fanciful, for we have little first-hand information. But this we do know: Van Gogh was more than a dedicated preacher. He slept in a bare room on a bed of hay, tended the sick and wounded and his self-sacrificial attitude stopped at nothing. He even ceased writing to Theo for over a year, because the latter had expressed some doubts about Vincent's work. But he did find time to read Shakespeare, Dickens and Victor Hugo and increasingly, to draw.

Something crucial must have happened to Vincent van Gogh in those months in the Borinage among the miners, but again, there are no letters to Theo to tell us what it was. But in July 1880 he emerged once again, this time in the mining village of Cuesmes where he wrote his most famous letter to Theo. The letter is a confession of faith in which he sets out for his brother an account of his entire life. The gist is clear: Van Gogh longs for Art: »When I was in other circumstances, where there were paintings and art objects, as you know, I conceived an enormous passion for that world, a wild enthusiasm. And I don't regret it, and still today, *far from home, I am often homesick for that land of paintings.*« Earlier that year he had walked seventy kilometres into France, because the painter Jules Breton whom he greatly admired, lived in Courrières. He saw Breton's house, but dared not knock on the door.

When he was writing the famous letter of July 1880 there was as yet no sign of a decision to dedicate himself entirely to painting and drawing. But a couple of months later the die was cast. In October 1880 Vincent van Gogh travelled from the Borinage to Brussels where he planned to study at the Academy of Art and learn the basic principles of drawing and painting. »I have moved…so that I can address the funda-mental issues.« Vincent was then 27. By way of comparison: at the same age Picasso had already left behind his Blue Period and his Pink Period.

'Last Sunday we went for a
delightful walk outside the city
along the side of the river Merwe'

Windmills at Dordrecht   1881

Boy with Sickle 1881

Michelangelo had completed his *Pièta* and was busily engaged on his *David*. But Vincent van Gogh signed on at the Art Academy of Brussels, made anatomical drawings and copies after Millet and Holbein.

In April 1881 he travelled from Brussels to Etten, where his father then had a living as minister. He had struggled for months wondering about his future but one thing was now clear: the oldest Van Gogh son was in the thrall of Art. He had talks with Tersteeg, his former boss at Goupil's, and introduced himself to Anton Mauve, one of the most famous painters of The Hague School. The latter received him kindly, and said he was particularly interested in Van Gogh's »own work«. Following this first contact, Van Gogh's hopes soon became fixed on Mauve and he looked forward to a return visit from him in Etten. No visit came however, although they did keep in touch. Vincent made sketches and drawings and waited for Mauve. In December 1881 he took the bull by the horns and suggested to Mauve that he (Vincent) come and spend a month studying under him in The Hague. »Mauve's response was: ›I had always suspected you were a bloody dull fellow, but now I see that is not so‹«, Vincent regaled Theo with this cheering news and continued to his brother, »And I can assure you that these direct words from M. afford me more satisfaction.« Vincent's journey through the »land of paintings« had begun.

'Today I made another drawing of
a man digging and then one of a man and
woman sitting by the fireside'

An Old Man Reading by the Hearth 1881

A Woman Sewing 1881

An Old Man Putting Dry Twigs on the Hearth   1881

In The Hague Van Gogh felt he was on the right course

Still Life with Straw Hat   LATE NOVEMBER–LATE DECEMBER 1881

Almshouse Man with an Umbrella 1882

'The woman has become as fond of me as a tame dove'

Sien with Cigar, Sitting on the Ground by the Stove   1882

'I had the idea of giving the same feeling to
the landscape as I had to the figures,
a kind of compulsive and at the same time
passionate fusion with the soil'

Tree Roots in Sandy Soil 1882

Carpenter's Yard and Laundry   1882

Church Pew with Almshouse Men and Women   1882

'Worked again portraying miners' wives carrying sacks of coal through the snow – watercolour'

Women Carrying Sacks of Coal   1882

Wild dog and gentle dove

In a letter from Vincent van Gogh to Theo, December 1883. »Dear brother, I feel how Father and Mother *instinctively* think about me. There is the same sort of tentativeness about accepting me into the house as they would have in adopting a large wild dog...It would get in everybody's way. *And it barks so loud.* In short, it is a filthy beast.«

The most eloquent writer could not have summed up Vincent's situation in the early 1880's more succinctly. Indeed, the famous Dutch novelist Willem Frederik Hermans once remarked that Van Gogh's letters are among the highest achievements of Dutch literature. »A filthy dog who barks too loud« is a perfect description of how Van Gogh must have appeared in 1883 after years spent as a virtual tramp. From the time of his resignation from Goupil's in April 1876, he had been a wanderer. In the space of seven years he lived successively in London, Dordrecht, Amsterdam, Etten, Brussels, Pâturages, Wasmes, Cuesmes, Brussels, Etten, The Hague and Hoogeveen. He sought for God but in vain. Following a quarrel on the matter of church attendance, at the end of 1881 even his parents barred him the door. And he had twice been in love.

If we assume that his affection for the London landlady's daughter Eugenie Loyer was not too serious a matter, then Kee Vos was Van Gogh's first great love. The couple met in 1881 when she was staying with his parents in Etten – Kee was Vincent's cousin and a widow. Writing about her to Theo he said, »There is something I have to tell you. ... I want you to know that this past summer I fell so deeply in love with Kee Vos, that the only way I can think of to describe it is by saying, ›It is as if Kee Vos is my alter ego, and I am the alter ego of Kee Vos,‹ and – that's

'It could well turn out to be a really authentic painting of peasants. I know that's what it is'

The Potato Eaters   EARLY APRIL 1885

'Looking at the drawing you see that the former profound misery is still there'

Sien's Daughter with Shawl   1883

what I've said to her.« But Kee rejected his advances – claiming that she was not yet over the loss of her husband. Shortly after this, during his first stay at Mauve's in The Hague, Van Gogh met Sien Hoornik. Early May 1882: »This winter I met a pregnant woman deserted by the husband whose child she was carrying. A pregnant woman on the winter streets of The Hague. She had to earn money – so you may imagine what she was doing.« He goes on to describe how she became his model and that in return he bought her medicines and cared for her. »The woman has become attached to me, like some tame dove. For my part, I could get married now, and what better partner could I find than her?«

But he didn't get married. Instead, Vincent and Sien »shacked up together« in The Hague and he shared the responsibility for her two children. Meanwhile he studied the first principles of art. Van Gogh was now determined to be an artist, indeed, he felt he was one already. This led to a quarrel with Mauve. »Mauve is offended because I said ›I am an artist‹ but I won't take this back because it's obvious I am, and that word in itself encloses the meaning of always being a seeker without ever finding perfection.« Vincent van Gogh had found a name for his journey.

Initially, however, he constructed the boundaries for this road. Before he embarked on his period in The Hague, while still with his parents in Etten, he was chiefly engaged in copying the masters, delving into the rich sources which he had first encountered at Goupil's. He regularly asked Theo in his letters of that time to send him prints that he could copy, mainly of (social-)realistic artists such as Jules Breton, Francois Feyen-Perrin and Millet, whose famous painting The Sower is probably the theme that Van Gogh copied most often. He also drew copies of works by Hans Holbein and Jacob van Ruysdael – the scale of his endeavours reveals his ambition.

Before long he began drawing from models. Having little money he was forced to use inexpensive models, generally peasants or labourers whom he would sketch as they went about their work. Thus *Boy with Sickle, An Old Man Reading by the Hearth,* or *A Woman Sewing* are typical examples of »work in progress«. The awkwardness of Van Gogh's earliest work has disappeared now but it is still too soon to speak of a distinctive style. If we can already detect signs of »the great Van Gogh« these are to do with the subject matter. As the quarrel with his parents about church attendance indicates, Vincent had by now given up the more fanatic aspects of his faith but it had not disappeared from his work. From his very first drawings of farm labourers he developed his own unique symbolism. If you study his work as a whole, you will notice that Van Gogh was one of the first painters to take the world around him as his subject matter. Yet at the same time he gives a little twist to that world so that you can only really understand his work if you know something of his early background and ideas about life. For Vincent, a man working the land is never just simply that; he is also a symbol of the labourer who must earn his bread with the »sweat of his brow«. Furthermore, for Van Gogh he is a reminder of the years in London and the Borinage. These workers also represented the simple life he so deeply yearned for.

In The Hague Van Gogh felt he was going in the right direction. After his disagreement with Mauve he worked more and more on his own or else with well-known painters such as Weissenbruch or Breitner. The next step in his career flowed naturally and logically from this: in August 1882 he painted his first works in oils. He'd already tried this in January, but stopped because he still felt too unsure of himself, »too hesitant in his drawing.« But now, seven months further on, Theo had visited him and, impressed by Vincent's achievement, had given him some extra money. Vincent immediately sticked up with: »a large box of watercolours for 12 tubes of watercolour paint,« acquired new brushes and provided himself with a supply of paints »large tubes (that works out cheaper than small ones)« he explained. Theo might otherwise think his brother was being a spendthrift.

One of Van Gogh's first paintings is Young Girl in a Wood dating to August 1882. It is a remarkable canvas, certainly in the light of his later work. We see a stretch of woodland by day, the trees in the foreground no more than stumps whose roots claw into the earth. On the left, beside a stump, stands a girl in a white dress and a red hat. With hindsight, this piece is strongly reminiscent of a painting such as *Tree Trunks with Ivy* from 1889, the difference being that in the latter the young woman has been replaced by the uncontrollable ivy plant that suffocates the world. The girl in all her youth and purity is a fine symbol for the spring morning of Vincent's career; at the same time she is the first in a long line of solitary figures inhabiting Van Gogh's canvases. Always solitary, and always journeying on.

Vincent remained in The Hague until 1883. He lived with Sien, practised making group portraits (such as the drawing *Church Pew with Almshouse Men and Women*) and experimented with chalk drawing. Although his artistic development progressed by leaps and bounds, his life did not grow easier. The responsibility for Sien and her children weighed heavy on him. All the more when Theo wrote in the summer that he'd had a financial setback. This news greatly affected Vincent. »Things are looking very black right now. If only there were just me, but it is the thought of the woman and the children, poor lambs, that one would wish to protect.«

In September 1883 Van Gogh made a dramatic decision: he left Sien. Not only was this emotionally very heavy, for his letters reveal how deeply he cared about the three of them; but the decision was also symbolic. Vincent van Gogh separated himself definitively from the social life most people enjoy, choosing for his art. To mark this choice he initially moved to the barren Dutch province of Drente but after three months went to Nuenen, in the southern province of Brabant, where his father had just been appointed minister. It was December 1883 and the »wild dog« had found a home. He was thirty and returned to where his parents were living.

It seems that Van Gogh only planned to stay in Nuenen for a couple of months, but this was to turn into two years. There were considerable ups and downs in the relations between him and his parents but the steady rhythm of family life did him good. He set up a studio in one of the out-houses of his father's house, and read a great deal of art history. At the same time, the everyday excitement provided him with a certain distraction. When in January 1884 his mother broke her leg, it was Vincent who nursed her. A young woman from Nuenen, Margot Begemann, confessed her love for him and they decided to get married. But they encountered so much opposition from both families that Margot tried to poison herself. It seemed as if problems continued to pursue Vincent.

Things become even worse when his father died unexpectedly in March 1885. Yet although this was a family tragedy, it appears to have had little effect on Vincent's work. In the spring and summer he drew and painted outdoors, as is evidenced by his beautiful but heavily symbolic *Lane of Poplars at Sunset*. During the autumn and winter he painted still lifes and drew from models. In the winter of 1884 he produced practically non-stop a series of almost seventy heads of peasants. »If I say I'm a painter of peasants that's the truth of the matter and you'll see this is really so as time goes on. That's where I feel at home. It's not for nothing that I've passed so many hours sitting musing by the fireside with miners and turf-cutters, with weavers and farm labourers,« he was to write to Theo in April 1885. To begin with, he painted mostly frontal views of people with a somewhat melancholy, fixed gaze, as in Head of a Woman. But some time in February up pop the first heads of peasant women, who, bent over their baskets, sit peeling potatoes. They play the overture to Van Gogh's first masterpiece, *The Potato Eaters*. Never again in his entire career would he work towards a painting with such care, making so many preliminary studies, in which all that he had been learning in his apprentice years came to fruition. The peasants grouped around a table, the light falling upon their caps and the faces emphasizing the sombre scene, Van Gogh has worked it all out and recorded it down to the last detail. »All winter long I have been holding the threads of this canvas [The Potato Eaters] and searching for its definitive pattern,« he wrote to Theo, »and should it now appear to be a cloth with a rough crude aspect it is nevertheless so that the threads were chosen with care and according to specific rules. And it may well turn out to be an *authentic painting of peasant life. I know that's what it is.*«

In a way the painting of *The Potato Eaters* concludes Van Gogh's Nuenen period. Although he remained in the village another six months,

In her youthful purity she is a
beautiful symbol for the fresh beginnings
of Vincent's career

Young Girl in a Wood   AUGUST 1882

'I've seen them weaving
at night by lamplight, a very
Rembrantesque effect...'

Loom with Weaver   MAY 1884

he made no other great works. He devoted his time to making studies of peasants in the countryside, or at the grain harvest, painting peasant cottages and, increasingly with the onset of autumn painting more still lifes, including a curious pair of birds' nests. Although it appeared to be less ambitious, this work was not of inferior quality: *Sheaves of Wheat* and *Autumn Landscape* are among the most beautiful canvases of his early work. It is worth noting that he wrote to Theo of *Autumn Landscape:* »I have never been so firmly convinced that I shall makes things that are good, that I shall succeed in mixing and applying my colours so that I achieve the effect I'm aiming for.« Indeed, we are struck above all when looking at *Autumn Landscape* by the sense of control, mastery of the paint and of the material. During this time in Nuenen Vincent van Gogh left behind him once and for all the pupil stage. Before him stretched his road, full of promise.

It became clear that his days in Brabant were drawing to a close. With Vincent's father dead, the Catholic authorities in the village began to gang up against the presence of this »foreign element«. The rumour spread through Nuenen that Vincent had made a girl pregnant. The village priest was so incensed that he was prepared to bribe the peasants who used to pose as models for Vincent, not to do so. Although initially the farming folk paid little attention to all this fuss and bother it gradually became more difficult for Van Gogh to find models. Combined with his wish to draw from nude models, this persuaded him in November 1885 to quit the Netherlands. He was never to return.

Peasant Woman Gleaning, Seen from Behind   1885

'What one might term the proper, decent
Dutch woman isn't such an appealing subject
either to paint or to think about'

Head of a Woman   November 1884–May 1885

'What I think about my own work is that the painting of the peasants eating potatoes (—) après tout that's the best thing I ever made'

The Potato Eaters, ink (lithograph) on paper   1885

Sheaves of Wheat July–August 1885

For Van Gogh a man working on the land is
also a symbol for the labourer who must earn
his bread with the sweat of his brow

Two Peasant Women Digging up Potatoes   AUGUST 1885

Autumn Landscape NOVEMBER 1885

Rich colours,
rich sunlight

It is winter 1885. Vincent van Gogh, 32 years old, travels to Antwerp – and becomes a student. Looking at his work today it seems hardly credible but on the cusp of 1885 and 1886 Van Gogh was still so unsure of his work that he felt he needed further tuition. But it wasn't only diffidence. Van Gogh wanted to take the large leap into the professional art world and for this the city of Antwerp was the perfect stepping-stone. For there he could draw from nude models. And there too he could see the work of Rubens, the northern king of colour.

For the first few weeks everything went well. Van Gogh found a room over a paint seller's and studied at the Academy. But gradually things began to go wrong. He was short of cash and often sick. He wrote to Theo, »What the doctor tells me is that it's essential I live better than I've been doing and that until I'm stronger, I shouldn't work. I know I've made things worse by smoking too much – something I did all the more because that way you're not bothered by your rumbling stomach.« At the end of February he took one of the Academy's internal exams – and failed. Van Gogh, painter of *The Potato Eaters*, was sent back to the beginners' class.

On about the first of March, to Theo's surprise, Vincent suddenly appeared in Paris. It seems rather an abrupt transition, but Van Gogh must have been thinking about it for some time. If ever there was an earthly city on the horizon to which this pilgrim artist could journey, then it was Paris. At the close of the nineteenth century Paris was the flaming heart of the artistic world. It was the centre of heated discussions on art, the place where new movements were born more swiftly than a bottle of wine could be downed. Artists streamed there from far and wide,

Interior of a Restaurant   SUMMER 1887

'Monticelli, who was a logical colorist (–) definitely brought too much intellect to bear on his work, as did Delacroix and Richard Wagner'

Roses and Peonies JUNE 1886

and met up in cafes and salons, where they debated endlessly and heatedly. In Paris art ogled and lured.

This was where Van Gogh had to be. He had come a long way in his development without anyone to help him but now he felt the need of impulses from outside. In Paris he could measure himself against his outstanding contemporaries, he could take stock of his position as artist, he could hone his provincial ideas.

And in Paris – was Theo.

Ironically, we have very little information about what with hindsight we know to be the most social period in Van Gogh's life. Our main source of information, his letters to Theo, dried up. The brothers lived in the same house, first Theo's tiny apartment on rue de Laval, and later on rue Lepic in Montmartre. Theo worked and earned the money while Vincent studied in Fernand Cormon's studio. His fellow student François Gauzi would later note: »When Vincent van Gogh appeared in Cormon's studio he wanted us to address him only by his first name and for a long while we didn't know his surname... Coming from a northern country he didn't care for the Parisian mentality; and the spiteful characters in the studio didn't fool around with him. They were a bit scared of him.«

All the same, Van Gogh soon made friends. He got to know Emile Bernard, who became one of his most loyal friends for the rest of his life, as well as John Russell and Henri Toulouse-Lautrec. Through Theo, who was then running a small branch of Boussod & Valadon, Goupil's successors, he met a large number of Impressionist artists. However, by the time Van Gogh arrived in Paris the movement was actually waning. Initially this disappointed him, for undoubtedly the picture of a Paris full of Impressionists had beckoned him from Nuenen with visions of rapture. He was later to write, »People have heard of the Impressionists, and have great expectations of them and... when you see them for the first time, the disappointment is tremendous.«

Before long, however, his appreciation returned, partly due to Theo's highly sensitive behaviour. In his gallery he had works by, among others, Degas, Monet, Renoir and Sisley and he introduced Vincent at the studios of Signac and Seurat. Together with other painters such as Guillaumin, Pissaro and Seurat they would hold discussions into the wee small hours in the cafés of Montmartre. For the first time the relationship between Theo and Vincent was one of cross-fertilization: Vincent was on an equal footing with the other artists and Theo was the art dealer whose task was to sell their work.

This isn't to say that the relationship didn't have its thorny side. Confined to a tiny apartment-cum-studio, the two brothers came to realize how fundamentally they differed in character. Theo was good-tempered, calm and collected and cheerful; Vincent impulsive, passionate and chaotic. The two clashed, more and more. Once, in a sombre moment, Theo wrote to their sister Wil: »No one wants to come here any more, because there are always scenes, and also he [Vincent] is so messy and untidy that the place looks anything but welcoming. (–) It is as if there are two people, one of them brilliantly gifted, sensitive and gentle and the other peace-loving [Dutch: *vredelievend*] and callous. They make their appearance alternately, so that first you hear one of them, then the other. (–) It's a pity he's his own worst enemy because he makes life difficult not only for others but also for himself.« Happily, the crisis between the brothers was soon resolved. Theo and Vincent »made it up«.

And a good thing too, because the year and a half that was to follow would be decisive for Vincent's career. Already when he was working in Nuenen, Van Gogh had become more and more interested in colour. He studied the theories of Delacroix and especially the idea of »complementary colours«. This states that a primary colour is seen at its best in the proximity of a mixture of the other two primary tones. Thus red would be complementary with blue plus yellow, that is, green. In the same way yellow is complementary with purple (red plus blue) and blue is with orange (red plus yellow). In a letter sent to Theo from Nuenen, Van Gogh cites Delacroix with approval saying »that in the case of colour it is not so much a matter of *couleur locale* as the ›tone‹ of the colour in relation to other colours.« This contrast of complementary colours is often found in Van Gogh's canvases. And here too it would seem that when we know his ideas on the subject we are able to appreciate his work and his world all the more.

But in Paris Van Gogh also found new inspiration in other artists. The most important of these was Adolphe Monticelli (1824-1886), a French-Italian painter who would probably be forgotten if Van Gogh had not frequently proclaimed him to be his major model. Van Gogh loved the way Monticelli applied thick layers of paint and his »vibrant colours«. He wrote later to John Russell: »He (Monticelli) offers us something passionate and immortal – he offers us the rich colours and the rich sunlight of the burning South like a true colorist, comparable with the way Delacroix wrote about the South, namely, that its quality should be presented by creating a simultaneous contrast of colours and their complementary tones and harmonies and not just by painting masses and lines.« It is as if Van Gogh is describing his own work.

Little of this can be detected in the paintings Vincent made during his first year in Paris. He worked in Cormon's studio, copying plaster models, drawing busts, cityscapes and the occasional still life. He explored the city. He painted a series showing the Moulin de la Galette, already immortalized by Renoir. And he remained sensitive to the changing seasons. During the cold French winter, which prevented him from working outdoors, and presumably because of shortage of cash, he painted several (flower) still lifes in which we clearly see that he hadn't yet freed himself from his northern sobriety. A still life such as *Roses and Peonies* is attractive, but the pink and green colours are so subdued that the picture looks as if it had been painted in a weaver's dwelling in Nuenen. Evidently, Van Gogh's self-confidence is still not sufficient for him to plunge into the Parisian colour orgy. First, he reconnoitres. Waits and watches. Bides his time.

A change may be detected when in the winter of 1886 to 87 he began a series of paintings using the cheapest and most readily-available model there was: himself. Shortly after his arrival in Paris he had painted a couple of self-portraits in Cormon's studio. Now they were to appear more regularly in his oeuvre, as if Van Gogh first tested every new discovery,

every technical skill he had mastered, on himself. The earliest self-portraits, dating from the autumn of 1886, are still dark and sombre but as
the season progresses, colour begins to burst through. A splendid example
of this is the famous *Self-Portrait with Grey Felt Hat*, in which, beneath the
dull grey jacket we detect a colourful blue cravat. The same necktie crops
up in the *Self-Portrait* from spring 1887. Here the background is green, Vincent's jacket is blue, trimmed with red piping. But even more striking is
the manner in which it is painted – it radiates an unprecedented swiftness of execution. Far more than the portraits that precede it, this one
reflects an almost nonchalant style of painting.

And then suddenly, in spring 1887 something seems to burst inside
Vincent van Gogh – or rather, breaks free. It has to do with the bursting
open of springtime colours but especially with developments in Paris.
Clearly, the Impressionists had gradually become part of the establish-
ment. Van Gogh considered himself and his friends as representatives of
the next generation. Indeed, he divided the Paris art scene into two
groups: the »old« Impressionists such as Monet, Sisley, Pissaro, Degas and
Seurat whose work hung in Theo's gallery on the boulevard Montmartre
and whom he named the 'Painters of the Grande Boulevard'. Then there
was himself and his kindred spirits Bernard, Gauguin and Toulouse-Lautrec,
who hadn't managed much more than to have their work hung in the
restaurant »Du Chalet« on the avenue de Clichy; he named this group the
»Peintres du Petit Boulevard«. The difference between the groups isn't
only a question of two generations. We find here a problem that bothered
Van Gogh from a far earlier date: to what extent is an artist dependent on
reality, or realism. Although the work of Impressionists such as Monet,
Manet and Degas represented a decisive break with the traditional realism
of the Romantics, they are still very close to Van Gogh. In Paris he was to
meet artists whose work was far more progressive. The canvases of Seurat
and Signac in particular, who with their technique of pointillism suggested the shimmering movement of light, had a profound impact on Van
Gogh. By placing different types of brushstroke side by side in a wide
range of tones, their canvases appear to vibrate and scintillate, dispersing

Through Theo, Vincent got to know the work of the Impressionists

Moulin de la Galette   OCTOBER 1886

The Hill of Montmartre   APRIL–MAY 1886

light like a sun-soaked summer's day. But it had little in common with what you actually saw. It appealed greatly to Van Gogh, who was later to write to Theo, »As for the pointillé, the ›aureole‹ or whatever you choose to call it, I think this is a great invention.« The word »aureole« already shows where the great appeal lay for Van Gogh. This can be seen most excellently in a painting like *Interior of a Restaurant*. The colours of the floor, the walls, the plants on the tables shimmer in the burning light as if the café is a bar in a baking desert where at any moment Clint Eastwood will come striding in. The world of Van Gogh's paintings breaks free from everyday realism.

And something else as well: in Paris, Van Gogh discovered a new Utopia. During the winter of 1886 he would spend hours, sometimes the whole afternoon, in Samuel Bing's printshop. Besides the thousands of bound books containing prints there was a sizeable collection of coloured woodcuts by Japanese artists such as Hiroshige and Kesaï Yeisen. From his meagre earnings Vincent regularly bought prints and encouraged Theo to do the same. Vincent was delighted by the quiet restraint of Japanese art, which tied in so admirably with his old longing for simplicity. For Van Gogh, Japan seemed the ideal Utopia – a distant land, but not impossible to reach.

Thus in the space of one and a half years, a new Van Gogh was born, who had in fact already been present within the old one. The combination of various things such as existing theories of colour, mixed with the atmosphere in Paris, influences from the Impressionists and pointillism, with the restraint and swiftness seen in Japanese art – all this in a short time shaped Van Gogh into a different artist. A painter who made canvases that shimmer with light. With the power and the skill to combine a surfeit of colours without their becoming one headache of superfluity. Above all, a painter who found the world he depicted on his canvases more real and significant than the one he observed around him. Looking at the paintings Van Gogh made after the summer of 1887 we can hardly fail to conclude that in an unbelievably brief period he had built up an astounding technical skill and assembled a wealth of subject matter. And he had still not reached the pinnacle.

Patch of Grass   APRIL–JUNE 1887

It was as if Van Gogh first tested on himself every discovery, every technical skill he acquired

Self-Portrait APRIL–JUNE 1887

Flowers in a Blue Vase   June 1887

'If Jeannin selected the peony and Quost the hollyhock, then indeed I have chosen the sunflower before anyone else'

Four Sunflowers Gone to Seed   August–October 1887

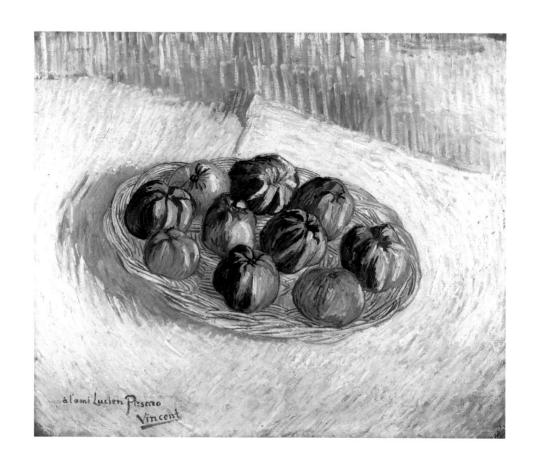

Basket of Apples SEPTEMBER–OCTOBER 1887

Still Life with Plaster Statuette LATE 1887

Waiting for
Gauguin

For Van Gogh had to journey on still further. If we recall his picture from the London sermon we might say that Paris was the city on the horizon. But having arrived there Van Gogh understood that he was not travelling to reach a destination – he was journeying for the sake of the journey. So he continued, towards the far horizon and immortality. His quest was embodied by the exotic and brightly shining land of Japan. In June 1888 he wrote to Theo: »As for living in the South, even if it's more expensive, look, we love Japanese art, it has influenced us – all the Impressionists have that in common – and then why not go to Japan, or in other words, what is the equivalent of Japan, namely the South?«

So it was that in February 1888 Van Gogh arrived in the south of France, in the town of Arles. It isn't clear why he chose this place, the first reference to it appears in a letter when he was already living there. But clearly, he wanted to get away from Paris. In June 1888 he wrote to his sister Wil: »We are now living in a painters world where it is indescribably dull and depressing. The exhibitions, the shops where paintings are sold, everything, but everything is overrun by bloated middlemen who intercept all the money and pocket the pickings.« What follows is even more pertinent: »People will pay a lot for a painting if the artist is dead. And the living artists are always pushed into the background and as it were beaten upon the head with the works of those who are no longer living.«

But there is another thing too: in the south of France Van Gogh is in search of colour. For many years his work and his milieu were in balance, but now that he has discovered colour he tries to find that in the world. This quest in turn uncovers a major source of suffering: in his

'I often have the feeling that the night is more full of colour than the day'

Terrace of a Café at Night (Place du Forum)   16 SEPTEMBER 1888

'The painter of tomorrow will be a colorist the like of which has never been seen'

Bridge at Arles (Pont de Langlois) MID MARCH 1888

endless struggle to grow and develop, Van Gogh has begun a search for a world that can no longer be found. His paintings have already become the representation of a Utopian dream, but in order to nourish this Utopia he needs a world to stimulate him in his work. So the journey continues. On and on. It seems a little naïve to attribute, as is often done, Van Gogh's increasingly wild outbursts on canvas to his disturbed mental state. Rather, they bear witness to an unquenchable desire for a Utopia that seems to become ever more unattainable. In Nuenen it was Paris, in Paris it was »the South«, and in the South it becomes – maybe heaven?

The more arduous and abstract the journey became, the more difficult it was for Van Gogh to travel on alone. In June 1888 he was to write to Theo: »I still believe the future of the new art to lie in the South. But it is not wise to stay here alone when two or three can help each other to survive on very little money.« That has a practical ring to it – two is cheaper than one. Money certainly played a role – and especially where Theo was concerned, for Vincent was financially dependent on him. But what Vincent needed above all was a colleague who believed in the same Utopia as he did. The fact that Vincent's work received no acclaim and was not selling certainly didn't improve the situation. So he continued with untiring requests attempting to lure Theo, Gauguin and Bernard to the south of France.

Meanwhile Van Gogh worked as one possessed. Ironically, when he arrived in Arles the town lay under sixty centimetres of snow and the glorious colours he had anticipated lay concealed beneath a thick white blanket. Despite this he was totally inspired by being in the South, the land of his dreams, and his work made mighty strides forward. In a brief study like this one, it seems absurd to invent new superlatives for the work Van Gogh produced in the summer of 1888 – he painted one master-piece after the other. In the south of France he finally dared to let go of reality. The personal »layers of meaning« that had always characterized Van Gogh's work now became more profound. And they coincided with each other: the images from Christianity, the complementary colour theory, the work of Millet, Delacroix, Monticelli and Signac. And Japan.

Increasingly, the outside world became an antechamber. Anyone who knows this part of France will recall how the dazzling light seems to absorb all colour from the world. Tempting as it may be to view the vibrant canvases from Arles as a reflection of what Van Gogh actually saw, anyone who believes this has been enticed – most successfully – into his Utopia.

His art, however, only gets better. Take *Pink Peach Trees* (*Souvenir de Mauve*) which he dedicated to his former, by then deceased, teacher in The Hague, Mauve; in the delicate beauty of its late-winter colouring it displays all the characteristics of a Japanese print. In *Bridge at Arles* (*Pont de Langlois*) and *Orchard Bordered by Cypresses* the blue shouts hosanna, the yellow sings arpeggios and the green pizzicatos passionately; the canvases he painted in the south of France are vibrant with *life* because Van Gogh projected onto them the envisioned world he so fruitlessly sought.

And Van Gogh went further. And further.

In June he made a little jaunt to the coastal village of Saintes-Maries-de-la-Mer, which produced three paintings and twelve drawings in one week. *View of Saintes-Maries-de-la-Mer*, the painting in the Kröller-Müller collection, would undoubtedly be hailed as a unique masterpiece – with its glorious bright colours – were it not painted by Vincent van Gogh. But by now his level and production were at such a peak they simply went from pinnacle to pinnacle. In those months he seems to have lived on a high, in an artist's glow of intoxication. In a couple of weeks he made another masterpiece: *The Sower*. In this sublime painting various themes of Van Gogh meet: the sower as the symbol for Christ; as the symbol of death and resurrection; and as a reference to Millet's work, one of Vincent's inspirations. Furthermore it is a symphony of complementary colour tones, the pairs yellow and purple, blue and orange. In the same month he paints *Wheat Stacks in Provence* – there's no stopping him.

Indeed, Van Gogh was now producing at such a rate that even he became suspicious. He continued to paint and draw (it was June, the corn fields stood ripe) and excused himself to Theo: »I think I should warn you that everyone will say I'm working too fast. Don't believe a word of it. Are we not led by a feeling, the truth of a feeling about nature, and if from time to time the feelings are so strong that you can work without noticing it (...) then you need to remember this hasn't always been the case and doubtless in the future there will come many heavy days without inspiration.« Prophetic words indeed.

All the time the longing for a companion, a fellow traveller, grew more intense. More and more Vincent writes about his own difficulties and mirrors himself on men of genius from the past and present. He would like to have some of the latter near him. During his first months in Arles Van Gogh lodged in a hotel by the station but in May he rented a small dwelling, known as the Yellow House. Immediately he began suggesting in his letters to Theo that, »If necessary two people could live in the new studio and I'd quite like that. Maybe Gauguin will come south. Maybe I'll be able to agree with MacKnight. Then we could make meals together.«

Not having enough money for the furnishings and because he had quarrelled with the landlord, Van Gogh initially moved to other lodgings. But he had set his heart on the Yellow House – he wanted to live and work there, preferably in an artists' colony. He pinned all his hopes on Gauguin. He had heard from Theo that Gauguin was living in Pont-Aven, that he was poorly off and frequently ill. Furthermore, he recognized Gauguin as an ally – for he too was a seeker-manqué. Vincent hoped through Theo to persuade Gauguin to come South.

When in June 1888 Gauguin made cautious noises about coming to Arles, Van Gogh was filled with a remarkable euphoria. In almost every letter he wrote then, whether it was to Theo or Wil, Gauguin's name pops up. »And next year when my friend Gauguin and I are sharing a house...« His old friend has become the Messiah who will redeem him from his loneliness. And who must be received with fitting ceremony. To lighten the burden of waiting for Gauguin, Van Gogh decided when in September he moved into the Yellow House, that he would paint a series of sunflowers. »In the hope of sharing a work place with Gauguin, I plan to make a wall decoration for the studio. Nothing but huge sunflowers.«

It seems fairly safe to say that the creative volcano that erupted from Vincent van Gogh during the summer of 1888, while he was waiting for Gauguin, knows no equal in art history. Today's viewer can scarcely conceive that in the space of two months Van Gogh painted the series of sunflowers, which after the *Mona Lisa*, are probably the most well-known paintings in the world. And not only that, but he went on to paint *The Night Café*, the famous red room with the sizzling yellow lamps. And the *Starry Night*, presently in the Musée d'Orsay. And the *Yellow House*. And *The Green Vineyard*. And the *Pavement Café at Night*...

Vincent worked and worked in those months making painting after painting, which are still considered to be among the very best in Western art. Meanwhile his moods swung backwards and forwards like a pendulum. He was alternately despairing, determined and downright angry. And he projected more and more expectations onto his friend. In mid September he sent Gauguin a self-portrait as a token of friendship. A couple of weeks later Gauguin returned the gesture, painting one of himself.

Then, on 23 October 1888, Paul Gauguin arrived in Arles. The two men were each slightly taken aback by the other. Van Gogh because Gauguin looked much fitter than he'd imagined. Gauguin, however, was to write later in a letter to Theo that Vincent seemed »somewhat excited«. Before long the roles were fixed. Gauguin was the dominant partner, telling exciting stories of his sailing adventures. Vincent was the adoring listener.

The same pattern emerged when they began to paint together. After a couple of days the pair of them went to the cemetery at Alyscamps, slightly south or Arles. The result of this session gives a clear indication of the balance of power: Gauguin worked in his familiar dry style, using matt, earthy muted tones. And Vincent – did exactly the same. It is almost painful to see how much the impassioned Van Gogh seems to copy his friend in their first days together. In particular *Falling Leaves (Les Alyscamps)* is a magnificent example of a – conscious or not – imitation on Van Gogh's part. With its perspective, its colours and its com-

'I thought that something in memory of Mauve should be at once delicate and very cheerful'

Pink Peach Trees (Souvenir de Mauve)   AROUND 30 MARCH 1888

'The cypresses have the beauty of
an Egyptian obelisk, when you think of
their lines and their proportions'

Orchard Bordered by Cypresses   APRIL 1888

paratively reserved style it is strongly reminiscent of Gauguin's work, especially his Vision after the Sermon.

It is soon clear that the two don't gel. The friendship is too unbalanced, too suffocating, expectations do not match and it could never lead to a fruitful collaboration. Little of this emerges from Van Gogh's letters. In December he is still writing to Theo, »(Gauguin) is a truly great artist and a most excellent friend.« But read in contrast what Gauguin had to say: »When I arrived in Arles Vincent was completely absorbed by the neo-Impressionist School and was in a real state of confusion. I took it upon myself to sort him out which wasn't difficult to do for I found a rich and receptive soil. From then on Vincent progressed by leaps and bounds; he seemed to uncover all that lay dormant within him.« It should be said, just to set the record straight, that this artist who seemed to be in such a confused state had just painted the *Sunflowers*, the *Night Café*, *Starry Night* and *Pavement Café at Night*, and these canvases were probably hanging on the walls where Gauguin was living. You'd be quite justified in asking which of the two had the more clouded perception of the world.

In the weeks that followed, the two men continued painting together. They made landscapes and portraits, including the one of Monsieur Ginoux, to which Vincent gave a splendid green background. They discussed matters together and noticed that their ideas on art diverged more and more. You don't need a profound understanding of human psychology to appreciate that this boiling cauldron would soon overflow – and that one of the two men would explode. Presumably Van Gogh. For months he had anticipated this collaboration with his 'saviour' but now Gauguin turned out to be just an ordinary man, domineering, somewhat conceited but also full of doubts and homesick for the north. More and more often, talks between the two artists ended up as arguments. Whether or not Vincent was suffering at this stage from a mental disorder, and if so to what extent, is difficult to determine.

In mid-December 1888 he wrote to Theo: »I believe Gauguin was a bit disappointed in the good town of Arles, in the Yellow House where we work and above all in me. (...) *Enfin*, I think he will either go for good or stay for good.« But in fact he already knows the answer. Gauguin is on the point of leaving Arles.

View of Saintes-Maries-de-la-Mer AROUND 2 JUNE 1888

'O how magnificent the sun is here at the height of summertime. It beats down upon your head and I'm absolutely sure it turns you crazy'

Wheat Stacks in Provence   AROUND 12 JUNE 1888

'The air is the colour of chrome yellow, fierce as the sun, which is chrome yellow I mixed with a little white while the rest of the sky is a mixture of chrome yellow 1 and 2. Brilliant yellow'

The Sower   17–28 June 1888

View of «La Roubine du Roi» with Washerwomen   1888

Path in the Park   AROUND 17 SEPTEMBER 1888

'O, my study of the vineyard – I sweated blood
and tears over it, but it's turned out a success;
another canvas measuring 30 square centimetres,
again to decorate the house'

The Green Vineyard   3 October 1888

'I'm pretty confident that we can count on Gauguin's staying with us permanently and that there will be no loss on either side'

Falling Leaves (Les Alyscamps) 1 NOVEMBER 1888

Portrait of Joseph-Michel Ginoux   FIRST HALF OF DECEMBER 1888

Still Life with a Plate of Onions   EARLY JANUARY 1889

'I'm working on **another model** now, a postman in **his blue uniform** with gold braid trimming, a powerful bearded head, **very Socratic**'

Portrait of Joseph Roulin FEBRUARY–MARCH 1889

'And if this canvas were to be hung just as it is in a fishing boat (–) I believe there would be people who would recognize it as a woman rocking a cradle'

'La Berceuse' (Portrait of Madame Roulin)   29 MARCH 1889

The Garden of the Asylum at St. Rémy   MAY 1889

'Wrestling through the dark night'

On 30 December 1888 a brief announcement appeared in *Le Forum Républi-cain*, a newspaper covering events in Arles and district. It read: »Last Sunday, at half past eleven at night, a certain Vincent Vangogh, artist, originally from the Netherlands, presented himself at the Brothel no.1. He asked for one Rachel and handed her his ear with the words, ›Look after this carefully.‹ Then he left. When the police were informed of this fact, that could only be the action of a poor demented person, they went to the man's house the following morning. He was lying on his bed almost lifeless. The unfortunate man was immediately admitted to hospital.«

Gauguin had his own interpretation of these events. According to him, he and Vincent had a discussion on the evening of 23 December, which ended up with Vincent's attacking him with a razor. Gauguin escaped from the Yellow House and spent the night in a guest house. It would seem that Van Gogh, in a fit of confusion, then grabbed the razor and cut off a piece of his own ear. When Gauguin went to the house the next morning, Vincent had already been found. Gauguin cabled Theo in Paris and the latter took the first night-train south. The two men travelled back to Paris on Christmas Day. Gauguin had not been to see Vincent in hospital.

So Van Gogh was alone again.

At first glance he seems to have recovered remarkably quickly. Already on 2 January he wrote a letter to Theo, primarily to set his brother's mind at rest. And he started working almost straight away. One of the

Olive Grove   JUNE 1889

'But quite honestly, my dread of going insane is much less than it used to be'

Enclosed Wheat Field with Rising Sun LATE MAY 1889

first paintings he made was *Still Life with a Plate of Onions* in which we can read clearly the title of the book *Annuaire de la santé* by F.V. Raspail, a work propagating ideas on a type of natural healing that appealed to Van Gogh. In those days Van Gogh also painted three portraits showing himself with his ear bandaged.

Happily, there were people around him. Looking back on that period, it is remarkable how well Van Gogh had analyzed life: the support he needed always came from »ordinary« people. His brother Theo was of course the prime example, but there was also »Father« Tanguy in Paris. Now, hospitalised in Arles, his guardian angels were Joseph Roulin, the local postman, and Roulin's wife Augustine. He showed his thanks to Roulin and his wife appropriately by painting a series of their portraits. The series showing Augustine became famous under the title *La Berceuse*, or woman rocking a cradle (also the French word for »lullaby«). In the painting she is holding a rope with which she rocks her child's cradle to and fro.

By this time the »old Vincent« had vanished for good. Van Gogh still worked on steadily but the manic activity of the second half of 1888 would never be repeated. On 28 January he wrote to Theo: »Just a short line to tell you my health and my work are progressing quite well. (…) I knew once upon a time that if you broke your arm or leg that would get better in time. But I never knew that you could be broken mentally and still heal. In my astonishment at a recovery for which I had not dared to hope, I find myself asking the question, ›What is the point of getting better?‹« This sense of weary doubt can also be seen in his paintings. For the first time in his life Van Gogh's work makes no progress; instead he looks backwards, almost as if it is consoling to meet old friends again. He paints a new series of sunflowers and several landscapes. And once more he makes copies after old masters.

But he will never be better again. On 7 February, by order of the district police commissioner of Arles, he is committed to a private cell in the hospital. Although on 17 February he is allowed to go home, less than ten days later he is back in the hospital. This is partly because of a petition delivered to the mayor by thirty »concerned citizens of Arles« in which they urged that the »insane red-headed man« (fou roux) be placed under lock and key. It was a painful parallel with Van Gogh's expulsion from Nuenen.

On 8 May Van Gogh had himself admitted to the mental hospital in Saint-Rémy, which was housed in the twelfth-century monastery of Saint-Paul-de-Mausole. Van Gogh was given two rooms, one to live in and one to work in. And since he is Vincent van Gogh, he immediately dashed off a masterpiece: the magnificently straggly *Irises* that was to be auctioned in 1987 for 49 million dollars, making it the most valuable painting in the world to date. However, *Irises* was not typical of his new work. If you look at Van Gogh's paintings made in Saint-Remy and later, in Auvers, you notice that the excitement and exuberance is somewhat curbed. Even a painting like *The Enclosed Field* is more restrained than normal. Incidentally, a new theme in Van Gogh's oeuvre appears in this work: the wall. It is as if, while in the asylum of Saint-Remy, Van Gogh understands that the end of his journey is approaching. No more huge horizons and endless distances; from now on many of his canvases would contain a wall, cutting off further view – it is hard to imagine a more definitive or poignant barrier.

But the walls also represent protection. The quest is past history for Van Gogh, who is now so great an artist that even his new restrictions can't put him down. *Wheat Field with Reaper* is a sublime symphony in yellow, Van Gogh's favourite colour. And the *Olive Grove* painted in June is an impressive canvas. While it may lack the wealth of colour found in his earlier works, the despairing groping branches are reminiscent of the doomed souls in Bosch's work, clutching at heaven. As far as emotional power is concerned, it has its equal only in the well-known *Starry Night* in which the stars sizzle through the night sky like burning comets.

This unflagging ability to continue painting did not mean things were getting any better for Van Gogh. He remained in an unbalanced state. What this implied in his case was not that he sank gradually into a bottomless pit but that he had mood swings – he would feel gloomy and depressed, and then at times remarkably calm, clear and contemplative. He wrote to his sister Wil in May: »Every day I taken a little of the medicine prescribed by the inimitable Dickens to ward off suicide. This consists in a glass of wine, a piece of bread and cheese and a pipeful of tobacco. (...) Ah well, it's not all fun and games but I try to remember to keep on joking, I try to push far away anything that would seem to resemble the heroic, the martyr's path.«

But it's not easy. In mid-July, while working on the picture *Entrance to the Stone Quarry* he has another attack and (intentionally) swallows a dose of poisonous paint. As a result, Van Gogh had to endure the most terrible bereavement that could overcome him. Doctor Peyron, concerned at his patient's unpredictability, forbade him to paint. Nor could he go outdoors. For almost a month and a half, Van Gogh could not work. He grew increasingly depressed during that period, especially since he began to understand that from then on the crises were likely to repeat themselves.

He gradually withdrew into a world of his own. When at the end of August he was allowed to paint again indoors he made a new series of self-portraits and even attempted a subject that until then he had kept well at arm's length – scenes on Christian themes. He painted two Piètas in the style of Delacroix and an angel after Rembrandt. Van Gogh's version is bathed in a light of brilliant blue.

Then, in September 1889, something totally unexpected. For the first time, whispers of praise from Paris. Van Gogh's *Starry Night* and *Irises* were exhibited at the fifth »Salon des Indépendants« in Paris. Shortly before this the critic J.J. Isaacson, living in Paris, had written the first laudatory words about Van Gogh's work. »Who is it that interprets for us in shapes and colours the magnificent, grand life that in our century people are experiencing with an ever greater self-awareness? I know only one, a pioneer, a lonely wrestler in the dark night, and the generations to come should brand his name upon their memories: Vincent.« And Vincent's reaction to this homage was most revealing; he wrote to Theo, »Needless to say I find it excessively exaggerated what he says about me in a brief notice.« But as the art historian Hulsker was to put it: Isaacson's words were like a herald's clarion call.

And indeed: during those months Vincent received more and more recognition. An enthusiastic article over his work came from the critic Albert Aurier. Furthermore, Van Gogh sold his first canvas: Anna Boch, the painter Eugene Boch's sister, bought *The Red Vineyard* for 400 francs. It was to be the only painting he sold during his life.

And Vincent withdrew even further.

He returned to Millet, his former love, and copied a series of peasants by him, or perhaps we should say, he translated them into his own style. When he was permitted to go outdoors once more, he plunged into the wooded autumnal landscape, with such works as *Windblown Pine Trees against a Red Sky*. By now, his work bears almost no trace of realism. »Especially now that I am ill, I try making something that will solace me, something I will like myself. I take as motif the black-and-white pictures by or after Delacroix or Millet. And then I improvise with colour,« he wrote to Theo.

At the end of December, about a year after the affair with Gauguin, he again took a dose of poisonous paint during an attack. The first paintings he made after this chiefly reflect his gloom and depression; they are autumnal scapes, caves, corridors in the asylum, sombre scenes that undoubtedly echo his sensitivity to the seasons.

Nevertheless, occasionally there was an exception. On 31 January Jo, Theo's wife, gave birth to a son whom they called after him: Vincent Willem. For his little nephew, Vincent painted the amazingly delicate *Blossoming Almond Branches*, which in their lightness and detail are unique in Van Gogh's oeuvre. Clearly, despite his growing weakness, he didn't lose his ability to paint, witness the two *Vases with Irises* (now in New York and Amsterdam) from May 1890, masterpieces of controlled painting which are among Van Gogh's very best work.

Slowly, with the coming of spring, things improved for Van Gogh. He undertook a journey to Paris and set off from there to Auvers-sur-Oise. This was the home of the doctor Paul Gachet, who was to be the

Wheat Field with Sun and Cloud   1889

'If I send you the 4 canvases of the garden that I'm presently occupied with, you'll see that — considering that life takes places mostly in the garden, it's not such a sad business'

Flowering Bushes in the Asylum Garden 1889

last friendly soul to help Van Gogh along his path. Besides being a doctor Gachet was an amateur photographer and he receives Van Gogh warmly – he was in many ways a kindred spirit. »I get the impression he is as sick or weary as I am myself,« Vincent wrote to Theo without any ironic overtone. »He is older than me and lost his wife a few years ago but he is a doctor through and through and his profession and his faith keep him going.« Vincent revived in Gachet's vicinity – so much so that the doctor's prognosis is: no more attacks. Van Gogh makes a final series of magnificent works: two portraits of Paul Gachet, *Field with Poppies, Sheaves of Wheat* and of course the famous *Wheat Field with Crows*.

      Considering the circumstances and the comparative peace of mind that Vincent seemed to have found, the events of 27 July 1890 do come as a shock. That evening Van Gogh returned to his room in the inn where he was staying, later than expected. He went straight to his room. One of the other guests went to look for him, and found Vincent lying on his bed, wounded by a gunshot. He had tried to kill himself but the bullet had ended up in his side. Dr Gachet was sent for immediately and in consultation with the local doctor concluded that it would be impossible to remove the bullet. Theo came over from Paris and sat with his brother at his bedside. Vincent van Gogh died at half past one in the night of 28 to 29 July. Theo was to write later, »He longed for death. When I was sitting beside him and told him we'd try to make him better and that we hoped in the future he'd be spared from these despairing moods, he answered, ›La tristesse durera toujours‹ (the sadness will last forever) – then I sensed what he meant. Shortly after that he grew short of breath and at one moment closed his eyes. Then a great quiet filled him and he lost consciousness.«

      The funeral was held on 30 July. Theo and his brother-in-law André Bonger were there, and Paul Gachet. Lucien Pissarro came over from Paris, as did Emile Bernard, Père Tanguy and several others. Gachet tried to make a speech, but was so overcome by emotion that he burst into tears. Vincent van Gogh was buried in the cemetery of Auvers, on the hill behind the old church in the midst of wheatfields at their most golden.

In the weeks and years that were to follow, the speculations around Van Gogh's suicide assumed inordinate proportions. It was suggested that he could no longer bear his loneliness. That he wanted to die when his work had reached its pinnacle. Even that he had done it so that his work would rise in value, thereby providing Theo and his young nephew with a secure adequate income. It would seem most probable that all these factors played a role, but chiefly that Van Gogh was spiritually exhausted. He had already taken poisonous paint on two occasions. He realized that he wasn't going to get better and in a fit of despair had turned the gun on himself.

»I should so like to make portraits,« he had written to Wil a few weeks before his death, »that would be an inspiration, a revelation to people living a hundred years from now. So I try not to paint as if I were making a photographic likeness, but to express the passion within a person, and in doing this I use our knowledge and modern tastes about colour as a means of expressing and projecting a character.« That century has been and gone. Van Gogh's portraits, still lifes and landscapes continue to be a daily revelation for many. Seldom can an artist have succeeded so well in what he aimed for. Vincent van Gogh himself may have left the world, but his colours and his images are painted passionately upon the sky. And they'll never fade away.

'The study is completely in yellow, thick clods of paint, but the motif was simple and beautiful'

Wheat Field with Reaper and Sun   LATE JUNE–SEPTEMBER 1889

Tree Trunks with Ivy   JULY 1889

'I wedged my easel with large stones (–) the drawing is tauter and has a kind of restrained passion'

The Ravine (Les Peiroulets) DECEMBER 1889

'The cypress is so typical of the Provençal landscape and you must have felt that when you said, "even the colour is black"'

Cypresses with Two Figures JUNE 1889–FEBRUARY 1890

The Sower (after Millet) JANUARY 1890

'Very glad that Gauguin thinks the painting in question of the Head of an Arlésienne is attractive'

The Arlésienne (Portrait of Mrs Ginoux)   FEBRUARY 1890

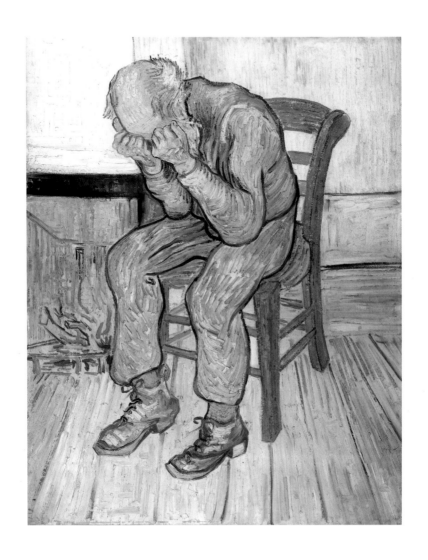

Sorrowing Old Man (At Eternity's Gate)   1890

'I've painted 2 canvases of the fresh grass in the park, one of which is simplicity itself'

Tree Trunks in the Grass   LATE APRIL 1890

The Good Samaritan (after Delacroix)   EARLY MAY 1890

'Very romantic, you might say, but also very Provençal, I think'

Country Road in Provence by Night   12 May–15 May 1890

Portrait of Dr Gachet   1890

Blossoming Chestnut Trees   22 MAY–23 MAY 1890

Portrait of a Young Woman   LATE JUNE–EARLY JULY 1890

Presented works

Presented works

p. 60 **Terrace of a Café at Night**
(Place du Forum)
16 SEPTEMBER 1888   oil on canvas,
80,7 x 65,3 cm   F 467, KM 108.565

p. 62 **Bridge at Arles (Pont de Langlois)**
MID MARCH 1888   oil on canvas,
53,4 x 64 cm   F 397, KM 111.056

p. 67 **Pink Peach Trees**
(Souvenir de Mauve)
AROUND 30 MARCH 1888   oil on canvas,
73 x 59,5 cm   F 394, KM 108.317

p. 68 **Orchard Bordered by Cypresses**
APRIL 1888   oil on canvas, 64,9 x 81,2 cm
F 513, KM 108.685

p. 70 **View of Saintes-Maries-de-la-Mer**
AROUND 2 JUNE 1888   oil on canvas,
64,2 x 53 cm   F 416, KM 106.327

p. 71 **Wheat Stacks in Provence**
AROUND 12 JUNE 1888   oil on canvas,
73,5 x 93 cm   F 425, KM 108.785

p. 72 **The Sower**
17–28 JUNE 1888   oil on canvas,
64,2 x 80,3 cm   F 422, KM 106.399

p. 73 **View of »La Roubine du Roi with**
Washerwomen« 1888   ink (reed pen) on
paper, 31,5 x 24 cm   F 1444, KM 112.856

p. 74 **Path in the Park**
AROUND 17 SEPTEMBER 1888   oil on canvas,
72,3 x 93 cm   F 470, KM 100.251

p. 75 **The Green Vineyard**
3 OCTOBER 1888   oil on canvas, 72,2 x 92,2 cm
F 475, KM 104.607

p. 76 **Falling Leaves (Les Alyscamps)**
1 NOVEMBER 1888   oil on canvas,
72,8 x 91,9 cm   F 486, KM 108.668

p. 77 **Portrait of Joseph-Michel Ginoux**
FIRST HALF OF DECEMBER 1888   oil on canvas,
65,3 x 54,4 cm   F 533, KM 103.189

p. 78 **Still Life with a Plate of Onions**
EARLY JANUARY 1889   oil on canvas,
49,6 x 64,4 cm   F 604, KM 111.075

p. 79 **Portrait of Joseph Roulin**
FEBRUARY–MARCH 1889   oil on canvas,
65 x 54 cm   F 439, KM 103.101

p. 80 **'La Berceuse' (Portrait of Madame**
Roulin) 29 MARCH 1889   oil on canvas,
91 x 72 cm   F 504, KM 109.725

p. 81 **The Garden of the Asylum at St. Rémy**
MAY 1889   oil on canvas,
91,5 x 72 cm   F 734, KM 101.508

p. 83 **Olive Grove**
JUNE 1889   oil on canvas, 72,4 x 91,9 cm
F 585, KM 104.278

p. 84 **Enclosed Wheat Field with Rising Sun**
LATE MAY 1889   oil on canvas, 73,5 x 91,5 cm
F 720, KM 106.596

p. 89 **Wheat Field with Sun and Cloud**
1889   ink (reed pen), charcoal and chalk on
paper, 47,5 x 56,6 cm   F 1728, KM 125.482

p. 90 **Flowering Bushes in the Asylum Garden**
1889   watercolour on paper, 61,2 x 46,5 cm
F 1527, KM 124.948

p. 93 **Wheat Field with Reaper and Sun**
LATE JUNE–SEPTEMBER 1889   oil on canvas,
73 x 92 cm   F 617, KM 101.173

p. 94 **Tree Trunks with Ivy**
JULY 1889   oil on canvas, 49,5 x 64,5 cm
F 747, KM 100.398

p. 95 **The Ravine**
(Les Peiroulets)
DECEMBER 1889   oil on canvas, 73,2 x 93,3 cm
F 661, KM 106.109

p. 96 **Cypresses with Two Figures**
JUNE 1889–FEBRUARY 1890   oil on canvas,
91,6 x 72,4 cm   F 620, KM 103.931

p. 97 **The Sower**
(after Millet)
JANUARY 1890   oil on canvas, 64 x 55 cm
F 689, KM 110.673

p. 98 **The Arlésienne**
(Portrait of Mrs Ginoux)
FEBRUARY 1890   oil on canvas, 65,3 x 49 cm
F 541, KM 110.202

p. 99 **Sorrowing Old Man**
(At Eternity's Gate)
1890   oil on canvas, 81,8 x 65,5 cm
F 702, KM 111.041

p. 100 **Tree Trunks in the Grass**
LATE APRIL 1890   oil on canvas, 72,5 x 91,5 cm
F 676, KM 100.189

p. 101 **The Good Samaritan**
(after Delacroix)
EARLY MAY 1890   oil on canvas, 73 x 59,5 cm
F 633, KM 104.010

p. 102 **Country Road in Provence by Night**
12 MAY–15 MAY 1890   oil on canvas,
90,6 x 72 cm   F 683, KM 108.488

p. 103 **Portrait of Dr Gachet**
1890   ink (etching) on paper, 18 x 15 cm
F ?, KM 116.945

p. 104 **Blossoming Chestnut Trees**
22 MAY–23 MAY 1890   oil on canvas,
63,3 x 49,8 cm   F 752, KM 105.479

p. 105 **Portrait of a Young Woman**
LATE JUNE–EARLY JULY 1890   oil on canvas,
51,9 x 49,5 cm   F 518, KM 106.498

Literature

- Brouwer, Ton de, Van Gogh en Nuenen,
  Venlo/Antwerp, 1998.

- Dorn, Ronald et al, De wereld van Vincent
  van Gogh, portretten en zelfportretten,
  Zwolle, 2000.

- Druick, Douglas W. en Peter Kort Zegers,
  Van Gogh en Gauguin, het atelier van
  het zuiden, ex. cat. Van Gogh Museum,
  Amsterdam, 2002.

- Gogh, Vincent van, De brieven van Vincent
  van Gogh, four volumes, by Han van Crimpen and
  Monique Berends-Albert, The Hague, 1990.

- Hulsker, Jan, Van Gogh en zijn weg,
  Amsterdam, 1977.

- Stolwijk, Chris and Richard Thomson,
  Theo van Gogh, ex. cat. Van Gogh Museum,
  Amsterdam, 1999.

- Walther, Ingo F. and Reiner Metzger,
  Vincent van Gogh, alle schilderijen,
  Groningen, 2001.

Colophon

Publication: Stichting Kröller-Müller Museum,
Houtkampweg 6, Otterlo, The Netherlands

Photography: Tom Haartsen, Ouderkerk
a/d Amstel, The Netherlands

Translation: Wendie Shaffer

Proof reading: Kate Williams

Bookdesign: Andreas Tetzlaff, Gerard Hadders
(Buro Plantage, Schiedam, The Netherlands)

Typesetting: Evert Ypma

Lithography and printing: Waanders Drukkers,
Zwolle, The Netherlands